PRESIDENTIAL PETS

PRESIDENTIAL PETS

NIALL
KELLY

ABBEVILLE PRESS PUBLISHERS

NEW YORK LONDON PARIS

This book is dedicated to my mother.
—N.K.

EDITOR: Constance Herndon
PRODUCTION EDITOR: Sarah Key
DESIGNER: Celia Fuller
PRODUCTION SUPERVISOR: Hope Koturo

Library of Congress Cataloging-in-Publication Data

Kelly, Niall.
Presidential Pets/ by Niall Kelly
p. cm.
Includes indexes.
ISBN 1-55859-302-0
1. Presidents—United States—Pets.   I. Title.
E176.48.K45 1992
973-dc20   91-39587

Front cover: Nixon's dogs Pasha, Vicky, and Timahoe before the White House (see pg. 90).
Back cover: Ford with Liberty in the Oval Office (see pg. 92).
Half title: President Warren Harding cuddling a child and the family dog.
Title page: Caroline Kennedy's ducks in the White House fountain.
Page 5: First Lady Lou Hoover with one of the family dogs.
Page 6: Lyndon Johnson and his beloved mongrel Yuki in performance.
Page 8: Betty Ford and daughter Susan's Christmas decorating interrupted by Misty, one of Liberty's puppies.

CONTENTS

GEORGE WASHINGTON
11

JOHN ADAMS
14

THOMAS JEFFERSON
14

JAMES MADISON
16

JAMES MONROE
17

JOHN QUINCY ADAMS
17

ANDREW JACKSON
18

MARTIN VAN BUREN
19

WILLIAM HENRY HARRISON
21

JOHN TYLER
22

JAMES POLK
23

ZACHARY TAYLOR
25

MILLARD FILLMORE
26

FRANKLIN PIERCE
26

JAMES BUCHANAN
27

ABRAHAM LINCOLN
29

ANDREW JOHNSON
31

ULYSSES S. GRANT
33

RUTHERFORD B. HAYES
37

JAMES GARFIELD
41

CHESTER ALAN
ARTHUR
41

GROVER CLEVELAND
42

BENJAMIN HARRISON
43

WILLIAM McKINLEY
46

THEODORE ROOSEVELT
49

WILLIAM HOWARD
TAFT
53

WOODROW WILSON
55

WARREN HARDING
57

CALVIN COOLIDGE
61

HERBERT HOOVER
65

FRANKLIN DELANO
ROOSEVELT
69

HARRY TRUMAN
71

DWIGHT DAVID
EISENHOWER
75

JOHN FITZGERALD
KENNEDY
77

LYNDON BAINES
JOHNSON
83

RICHARD NIXON
89

GERALD FORD
93

JIMMY CARTER
96

RONALD REAGAN
98

GEORGE BUSH
101

LIST OF PETS
104

INDEX
107

GEORGE WASHINGTON
THE FIRST FIRST PETS, 1789–97

As a Virginia plantation owner, George Washington was devoted to animals and surrounded himself with them throughout his life. Indeed, one of his greatest contributions to the new American nation was to create a line of "supermules" to help him with his farm work at Mount Vernon. Since a mule is a cross between a jackass and a mare and is itself sterile, in order to create the superb mule he envisioned, Washington needed to introduce the finest jackass to mate with his mares. So when the king of Spain heard of the president's search he decided to present him with two of the best Spanish jackasses available.

Only one jackass landed safely in Boston, and Washington planned the animal's march south as carefully as he had planned any of his military campaigns. To ensure that all the mares were eager and ready, he deprived them of the company of his Arabian stallion, Magnolio, for weeks in advance. When the jackass arrived, Washington named him Royal Gift and set him loose with the mares. But to the president's chagrin, Royal Gift resisted their equine charms. Frustrated in his attempts at genetic engineering, Washington wondered whether the Spanish king had sent him an impotent jackass or whether the royal beast was simply too aristocratic to dally with republican American mares. As the Father of Our Country noted sarcastically in his diary: "His Most Catholic Majesty surely could not proceed with more deliberation and majestic solemnity to the act of procreation."

Left, surrounded by devoted dogs and happy family, George Washington bids farewell from Mount Vernon to the Marquis de Lafayette, 1784. A great friend of the United States, Lafayette presented dogs, including these two, to the country's first five presidents.

One of George Washington's favorite mounts was a horse named Nelson, seen here accepting Cornwallis's surrender at Yorktown, the battle that brought the War of Independence to an end.

Eventually the ingenious George solved the problem with a bait-and-switch routine, tantalizing Royal Gift with a female jackass and at the very last moment substituting one of the mares. In order to placate the Spanish beast, he sometimes allowed it to mate with the female jackass, thus producing a steady supply of young jackasses. These were sent on tours to improve the stock of jackasses throughout the new republic, providing the basis for the strain of fine mules found in the United States even today.

In addition to farm animals, Washington owned many dogs, which he gave such delightful names as Taster, Tipler, Forester, Vulcan, Sweetlips, Searcher, and Madame Moose. The latter was apparently a rather demanding pet. At one point when Washington was given yet another dog, he wrote in his diary: "A new coach dog [has arrived] for the benefit of Madame Moose; her amorous fits should therefore be attended to." The Marquis de Lafayette also sent Washington a pack of French hounds, but they proved to be so vicious that a huntsman had to be employed to supervise their mealtimes lest they tear each other to shreds over dinner.

Another important member of the Washington household was a green parrot, doted on by Washington's wife, Martha, and her granddaughter Nellie Custis. In a letter to a friend, Nellie gushed: "I have spent ten days most agreeably teaching our pretty green pet to sing 'Pauvre Madelon.'" But even an animal lover like Washington sometimes lost patience with the resident pets. In a letter describing his departure from Philadelphia at the end of his presidency he remarked: "On the one side I am called upon to remember the parrot, and on the other to remember the dog. For my own part I should not pine much if both were forgot."

As a young man, legend has it that George Washington planned to leave home for the high seas. In this etching of his attempted farewell, his faithful dog—backed up by both human and animal family members—convinces the future first president to stick around.

JOHN ADAMS, (1797–1801), was the second president of the U.S. and the first to live in the White House. While little is known about Adams's pets, he was responsible for building the presidential stables, where he kept his favorite horse, Cleopatra.

T H O M A S   J E F F E R S O N
THE RIGHTS OF ANIMALS, 1801–9

The father of the Declaration of Independence, Thomas Jefferson also believed in the rights of animals and allowed all creatures to live in peace at Monticello.

T homas Jefferson held the same democratic principles about animals that he did about humankind. He allowed all creatures to live in peace on his estate, and peacocks, pheasants, and partridges found refuge in the forests around Monticello. The father of the Declaration of Independence even trained a herd of deer to eat corn from his pockets.

When Jefferson became president, he sent Meriwether Lewis and William Clark on their famous expedition to explore the West. Among the things they brought back were several grizzly bears. These they presented to the president, who was so captivated by the animals that he built them a cage on the grounds of the White House and sometimes promenaded them around the garden. Attempting to ridicule his strange choice of pets, Jefferson's political opponents, the Federalists, dubbed the White House grounds "The President's Bear Garden."

However even a democrat like Jefferson had occasional lapses and liked some creatures better than others. Throughout his lifetime he showed a distinct preference for mockingbirds and owned several. In a letter to his daughter Martha, he waxed poetical about their song: "I sincerely congratulate you on the arrival of the mockingbird. Learn all the children to venerate it as a superior being in the form of a bird, or as a being which will haunt them if any harm is done to itself or its eggs."

Among Jefferson's mockingbirds arose one special favorite, a bird named Dick who became the president's constant companion. Dick's cage hung among the roses and geraniums in a window recess at the White House. Whenever the president was alone he opened the cage and gave Dick the freedom of the room. The bird would sit on the table and sing or would perch on the president's shoulder and take food from his lips. He also learned to imitate the call of other birds as well as cats and dogs, and Jefferson even trained Dick to accompany him when he played the violin.

On returning to Monticello at the end of his term as president, Jefferson noted with satisfaction in his diary: "My birds arrived here safely, and are the delight of every hour." Dick lived on at Monticello for many years and at the end of every day when the president retired to bed, Dick hopped up the stairs after him, one step at a time.

During Jefferson's lifetime Monticello was a haven for all sorts of birds and animals including peacocks, which were given the run of the estate.

JAMES MADISON
BIRDS OF A FEATHER, 1809–17

James Madison was the original wimp president, but he consorted with two colorful companions: his statuesque wife, Dolley, who often wore elaborate feathered turbans, and an equally dazzling family parrot. During the War of 1812, United States troops were defeated at Bladensburg, Virginia, by the British, who then marched on Washington. Dolley took flight, but only after saving the Declaration of Independence and the parrot. She gave the bird to her servant Jean Sioussat, who took it to the French ambassador's residence, Octagon House, where it remained in safety while the British burned Washington.

After the British departed, James Madison was reunited with Dolley and the parrot, and the three spent the rest of the presidential term at Octagon House. When James Madison died in 1836 the parrot was still alive, and is rumored to have outlived Dolley as well, who died in 1849.

During the War of 1812, Dolley Madison was forced to flee the White House with the Declaration of Independence and her parrot. The family's sheep had wisely stayed home at Montpelier (right), the Madisons' Virginia estate.

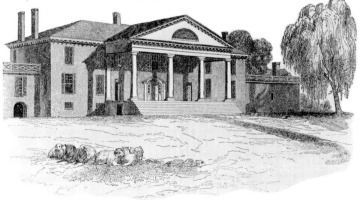

JAMES MONROE (1817–25) was fifth president of the country and originator of the Monroe Doctrine, whereby European powers were discouraged from intervening in the affairs of the American hemisphere. While not renowned for his animal connections, Monroe did own two sheepdogs, gifts from the Marquis de Lafayette. During their White House years his daughter Hester Maria also owned a small black spaniel to which she was devoted.

J O H N   Q U I N C Y   A D A M S
A WALK ON THE WILD SIDE, 1825–29

John Quincy Adams, sixth president and reluctant alligator host.

John Quincy Adams appeared to the world as a dry, cold politician, but his presidency saw some of the most exotic animals ever to live in the White House. In addition to the silkworms reared by Adams and his wife, Louisa (the First Lady spun the silk herself and is said to have made enough to create a number of her gowns), the family also hosted an alligator. The true patron of the alligator was the ubiquitous Marquis de Lafayette, who toured America during 1825. By the time he arrived at the White House, he had been given an alligator by some particularly generous citizen, and for several months it took up residence in the East Room. Finally in August, following an emotional farewell ceremony in the White House, Lafayette and his alligator departed.

ANDREW JACKSON
ANIMAL PLEASURES, 1829–37

The era of the aristocrats came to an abrupt end when Andrew Jackson was elected president in 1828. Old Hickory had been born in a log cabin and he prided himself for his plain speech and simple ways. Indeed, so attached was he to his rustic past that when he moved to Washington, D.C., he brought along his finest fighting cocks from Tennessee. These he proceeded to match against the local Virginia fighters, which unfortunately defeated the Tennessee birds. Undeterred, Jackson brought up several more pairs, but they too met with defeat. In this respect, the seventh president always said, his administration was a lamentable failure.

At the track Jackson had more success. A keen fan of racing, he kept the White House stables well stocked and entered his favorite fillies—Emily, Lady Nashville, and Bolivia—in many local races. Jackson's horses often galloped away with the prize money, but despite their success he always registered them under the name of his stepson, Andrew Donelson, fearing that it would be considered improper for the president of the United States to keep race horses.

The pet that was closest to Jackson's heart, however, was a parrot called Poll. The bird had been found in a Nashville confectionery shop and so impressed Jackson that he talked the owners into selling it to him. When he went to Washington to assume his presidential duties, Poll stayed behind in Nashville, but despite the many cares of state Jackson always found the time to

A great lover of horses, Andrew Jackson kept racing fillies in the White House stables and entered them on the sly in local races.

inquire after the bird's welfare in his letters home. At the end of his term, Old Hickory was reunited with Poll in Nashville, where the president died shortly thereafter. But eternal rest was to elude him for a little longer. While family and friends gathered for the funeral service, Poll watched from his perch, and as the solemn ceremony began he started to scream obscenities at the assembled mourners. Poll was hastily removed from the room, never to see his teacher and master again.

MARTIN VAN BUREN
THE FOX AND THE TIGERS, 1837–41

Sly Martin Van Buren was known to friends and foe alike as the Kinderhook Fox (after his birth place in New York), but even this accomplished politician lost a few battles with Congress. Shortly after he took over as chief executive, a ship arrived laden with gifts for the president of the United States from Kabul al Said, the sultan of Oman. Among the gifts was a pair of tiger cubs. Before Van Buren could decide how to accommodate these new pets in his household, Congress stepped in, insisting that the ship had embarked while Jackson was president and that therefore the cubs were the property of the people of the United States. With Van Buren arguing that they were sent to the president and were therefore his, the debate raged back and forth, but Congress won the day—the cubs were confiscated and sent to the zoo.

WILLIAM HENRY HARRISON
OLD TIPPACANOE AND THE
ANIMALS, TOO, 1841

Although William Henry Harrison had been born in a Virginia mansion, during his campaign he portrayed himself as an old farmer, and a log cabin became the symbol of his presidential crusade. Once in the White House Harrison kept up the old farmer act, and one of his first executive decisions (one of his last as well, since he died of pneumonia a month into his term) was to acquire a new cow for the White House. Shortly after his inauguration he set off for the cattle market where he bought a cow called Sukey from a Montgomery County drover. As they walked Sukey to her new home the drover plied Harrison with questions, but the president concealed his identity. Finally on arriving at the White House Harrison invited the drover to breakfast, but when the drover saw the fine repast laid out in the State Dining Room he could restrain his curiosity no longer and insisted on knowing his cow customer's name. "The people call me William Henry Harrison, and have made me president of the United States," the hero of Tippacanoe announced—at which point the drover bolted from the house and abandoned Sukey to her new presidential owner.

William Henry Harrison's presidential campaign relied heavily on rustic appeal, Harrison portraying himself as an old farmer straight out of a log cabin. In this election-era lithograph, the candidate and his dog are shown greeting an old soldier. According to its caption ". . . not only does the brave old Hero give his comrade a hearty welcome, but his dog recognizes him as an old acquaintance, and respects the welcome by a cordial and significant shake of his tail! If the looker will only watch close enough he can see the tail absolutely shake in the picture, particularly in a clear day."

Delighted with his new marriage, John Tyler tried to match up his canary with a mate, but when the bird took one look at his chosen consort he lay down and died.

J O H N   T Y L E R
THE MATING GAME, 1841–45

Following William Harrison's demise, John Tyler became the first vice president to assume office on the death of a president. Doubly dogged by tragedy, shortly afterward his wife died as well. A few months later, however, the resilient middle-aged widower fell in love with beautiful young Julia Gardiner. For months he pursued Julia with proposals of marriage until she finally accepted. To celebrate this joyous occasion, President Tyler imported a pair of Italian wolfhounds, who became a familiar sight as they romped on the White House lawn.

Their marriage proved so successful that the Tylers decided their canary Johnny Ty should also wed, so Julia wrote to her family in New York asking them to select a wife for the bird. When a suitable consort was found it was shipped by steamboat to Richmond and then by carriage to Sherwood Forest, the Tylers' home in Virginia. The delighted couple placed the new bride in the cage with Johnny Ty, but to their consternation Johnny immediately jumped off his perch, sat on the bottom of the cage, and hid his head under his wings. Within a week Johnny Ty was dead. Distraught, the Tylers took a closer look at his widow and found to their astonishment that they had married him off to another male.

In addition to the dearly departed Johnny Ty, Tyler enjoyed a close relationship with a horse called the General. When his mount died, the president buried him under the south lawn at Sherwood Forest within sight of his bedroom window and wrote an epitaph that was carved on the General's headstone: *Here lies the body of my good horse, The General. For years he bore me around the circuit of my practice and all that time he never made a blunder. Would that his master could say the same—John Tyler.*

Although few tales survive of **JAMES POLK**'s (1845–49) presidential pets, he must have been a familiar of the animal kingdom for he grew up on a North Carolina farm where, legend had it, he learned to ride as soon as he learned to walk.

James Polk, eleventh president of the United States and infant equestrian.

ZACHARY TAYLOR
OLD ROUGH AND READY, 1849–50

Zachary Taylor earned the nickname "Old Rough and Ready" during his long career as a soldier, and since most of his adult life was spent on military campaigns, his closest companions were his horses. Old Whitey was Taylor's favorite mount, although neither one cut a fine figure. The horse was actually grayish-white with a shaggy mane and knock knees. Taylor himself had a large equine head and his legs were so short that an orderly had to help him into Old Whitey's saddle. In the midst of battle Taylor sat with his leg thrown over the pommel surveying the action. As phlegmatic as his master, Old Whitey never flinched on the battlefield, but while lethargic by nature, he came to life during a parade and pranced in time to the music.

When Zachary Taylor was elected president, Old Whitey accompanied him to Washington and grazed on the White House lawns. But his well-earned rest was not without irritations, since it became a tradition among White House visitors to pluck hairs from his tail as souvenirs. Fortunately—or unfortunately, from a presidential point of view—his torment did not last, for after just sixteen months in office Taylor died and was buried with great pomp and ceremony. His body was carried in a sumptuous funeral car draped in black silk, with Old Whitey led directly behind, the boots of his dead master turned backwards in the stirrups.

Although neither one cut a fine figure, a horse called Old Whitey was Zachary Taylor's favorite mount. So devoted was the president to Old Whitey that he brought him along to the White House, where the horse grazed on the lawn and endured the torments of visitors.

No one expected vice president **MILLARD FILLMORE**
(1850–53) to become president, but when Zachary Taylor's death
put Fillmore in charge, slave owners rejoiced because his lack of
sympathy for the enslaved was well known. Indeed he seems to
have shown greater concern for animals than for his fellow human
beings. Though little is known of his own pets, Fillmore was a
founding member and president of the Buffalo chapter of the
American Society for the Prevention of Cruelty to Animals.

*America's thirteenth and fourteenth
presidents, Millard Fillmore and
Franklin Pierce.*

During his stay in the White House no animals are known to have
enlivened the life of **FRANKLIN PIERCE** (1853–57), whose third
and youngest son died shortly after he became president.

JAMES BUCHANAN
BUCHANAN AND THE BEASTS, 1857–61

James Buchanan was the only president who never married, a condition that inspired friends and political associates to send him animals as companions. The king of Siam presented him with a herd of elephants, but Buchanan wisely donated them to the zoo. On a slightly less ambitious scale, he also received a pair of bald eagles from a friend in San Francisco. These majestic birds strolled around the grounds of Wheatland, Buchanan's Pennsylvania home, and at night they slept in twin cages on the back porch. "These birds of Jove, as if conscious that they nestled beneath the eye of the Chief Magistrate of this great Republic, seem to plume themselves on their associations," wrote a visitor, "and although apparently as free as when at home on the Sierra Nevada, show no disposition to wing their flight from Wheatland."

While the eagles stayed home at Wheatland, Buchanan took his Newfoundland, Lara, to the White House with him. Remarkable for his enormous tail and his total devotion to his master, Lara became famous in Washington for his ability to lie in one pose for long stretches of time, one eye open and one eye closed.

ABRAHAM LINCOLN
DOGGED BY TRAGEDY, 1861–65

An air of tragedy seems to have hung over the Lincoln animals and more than a few of them met with sad ends. As a child, Abe formed a close but doomed relationship with a pet pig, which he taught to play hide-and-seek; later, when it grew to its full size, he rode on its back. But this beloved animal ended up on a plate with scrambled eggs, a turn of events that affected Lincoln so deeply that throughout his life he often reprieved animals otherwise destined for the table.

Ever the indulgent father, Lincoln allowed his sons to have as many pets as they wanted. At the White House, Tad and Willie started to accumulate a menagerie, including two ponies on which the boys soon spent their days riding around Washington. When the president reviewed the troops, his sons put on old military capes and rode out with him. But tragedy struck and Willie died suddenly of typhoid fever. A disconsolate Tad never rode again, claiming, "The ponies make me miss Willy even more." One night exactly two years after Willie's death, a fire broke out in the stables and the unfortunate ponies perished in the inferno.

Lincoln tried to cheer Tad with new pets. When someone in Philadelphia sent a pair of white rabbits, the president wrote: "Allow me to thank you in behalf of my little son for the present of white rabbits. He is very much pleased with them." But Abe was being less than honest; Tad took no interest in the rabbits and continued to pine.

Happily, a few months later Tad saw an animal that piqued his interest—a goat. A pair was immediately bought for him and he named then Nanny and Nanko. Although Mary Lincoln objected,

Abraham Lincoln with his son Tad and one of the family's two ponies. Both ponies died tragically in a fire, an event that is reported to have reduced Lincoln to tears.

Tad's goats were given the freedom of the White House. The First Child would hitch them to a chair and race his makeshift chariot through the corridors of power. Once when Mary took Tad to New York on one of her many shopping sprees, trouble almost struck again: "Tell dear Tad poor Nanny Goat is lost, and Mrs. Cuthbert and I are in distress about it," Abe wrote to Mary. "The day you left Nanny was found resting herself, and chewing her cud, on the middle of Tad's bed. But now she is gone!" But Nanny knew where her bread was buttered. By the time Tad returned to Washington, she was back at the White House.

As Lincoln's letter suggests, Tad wasn't alone in his affection for the two goats. One day when the president was setting out for a visit to the Washington Soldiers' Home, he piled Tad and Nanny and Nanko into the carriage with him. When a shocked presidential aide suggested that perhaps the goats shouldn't ride in the carriage, Lincoln shrugged, "Why not? There's plenty of room in here." So the goats rode in the carriage and the aide stayed behind.

One Lincoln pet who fared better than many others was Jack the turkey. Jack was originally presented to the White House as Christmas dinner, but in the weeks before the holiday Tad grew attached to the bird and pleaded with his father to spare it. As usual, Lincoln relented, and the tender bird became part of the presidential household. On Election Day 1864, while the Civil War raged close to Washington, a special booth was set up on the White House grounds so that soldiers serving nearby could vote. Lincoln, his private secretary Noah Brooks, and Tad were watching from an upstairs window when they saw Jack strut out among the voters. "Why is your turkey at the polls? Does he vote?" Lincoln asked his son. "No," Tad shot back. "He's not of age yet."

A N D R E W   J O H N S O N
OF MICE AND MEN, 1865–69

Andrew Johnson succeeded Abraham Lincoln to the presidency upon the latter's assassination.

Andrew Johnson was a farmer at heart, and when he became president after Lincoln's assassination he brought along his two Jersey cows to the White House. Despite the suddenly elevated status of the family, Johnson's daughter Martha rose at dawn every day to supervise their milking herself. But their bucolic lives were disturbed in 1868 when Congress began impeachment proceedings against Johnson because he had dismissed a cabinet member without the Senate's approval. Still, even in those dark days while he awaited the verdict of the hearings, Johnson was kind and considerate to little creatures. One evening he drew his secretary, William Moore, aside and shared a secret with him. The previous night the president had found mice playing in his room and had left a handful of flour for the little creatures. "I am now filling their baskets for them tonight," he confided. The next day Moore asked Johnson about his rodent friends. "The little fellows gave me their confidence," the president answered. "I gave them their basket and poured some water into a bowl on the hearth for them."

Ulysses S. Grant and family pose in front of the White House with a few of their pets—horses and ponies, all greatly loved, and one of the family's dogs. Many of the Grant dogs died under mysterious circumstances until the president threatened to fire the whole White House staff if another fatality occurred.

ULYSSES S. GRANT
FRIENDS OF THE GENERAL, 1869–77

Like all soldiers, Ulysses S. Grant was a great lover of horses and during his presidency the White House stables became home to many, including Reb and Billy Button; two mares named Jennie and Mary owned by his daughter Nellie; a pair of Shetland ponies belonging to his sons Jesse and Buck; Grant's old wartime mount, the pointedly-named Jeff Davis; Cincinnatus, a magnificent horse given to the president by the grateful citizens of Cincinnati; and a team of matched bays named Egypt and St. Louis.

So deep was Grant's love of good horse flesh that he continued to acquire even more of the animals. One day while out riding, a butcher wagon overtook him and Grant raced to catch up, passing the wagon while it was making a delivery. But within minutes the butcher wagon passed him again. Impressed by the butcher's horse, Grant followed the wagon to his shop and bought the horse for $280, no small sum over a century ago. Renaming it Butcher Boy, the horse became one of his favorites.

Grant's son Jesse was as fond of domestic pets as his father was of horses. He acquired several dogs after arriving at the White House, but they all died mysteriously. So when he was given a Newfoundland pup named Faithful, President Grant summoned all the White House staff and announced in his sternest military tones, "Jesse has a new dog. You may have noticed that his former pets have been peculiarly unfortunate. When this dog dies every employee in the White House will be at once discharged." Not

Ulysses S. Grant, daughter Julia, and one of the surviving dogs.

Grant's legendary horse Cincinnatus, which he received from the grateful citizens of Cincinnati during the Civil War.

surprisingly, Faithful lived to a ripe old age, and so did other dogs that Jesse later acquired.

Jesse also owned several birds, including a parrot given to him by the Mexican minister, Matías Romero. According to Jesse, the bird had few accomplishments: with no speech and no great beauty, it was noted only for the vileness of its temper. "One might have imagined him nurtured on chili peppers," he remarked. The parrot remained a part of the Grant household for a few years until it was passed along to friends. Many years later Jesse discovered that the bird was still alive, having been passed from one family to another as each one grew tired of it.

Grant's son kept two gamecocks as well, at first in adjoining yards on the White House grounds. But the birds fought constantly between the pickets until they were separated at opposite ends of the property, where even then they continued to disturb Washington's peace by crowing defiance at each other day and night.

Grant was once fined by a policeman, who did not recognize the president, for racing his horse through the city streets.

RUTHERFORD B. HAYES

NOAH'S COLLECTION, 1877–81

Rutherford Hayes and his wife brought an air of moral austerity to Washington, Lucy Hayes even earning the nickname "Lemonade Lucy" because she refused to serve alcohol at White House parties. Strict as these austere characters were, however, they easily opened their hearts to animals and kept many pets. Lucy referred to them as her "Noah's collection," although she did not insist that they come in pairs. Lucy's ark was home to one goat, four canaries, two hunting pups, two shepherd dogs named Hector and Nellie, one English mastiff named Duke, four kittens, and one mockingbird. President Hayes surveyed this scene with satisfaction. "Scott's new goat is a success—he hauls Scott all around," he wrote, referring to one of his grandchildren's pets. "The two dogs suit him too. Your mother's cat, dog, and mockingbird give a Robinson Crusoe touch to our mode of life."

Lemonade Lucy's love of animals soon hit the headlines and eventually the news even reached the U.S. consul in far-away Siam, a man named David Sickels. Perhaps hoping for a better posting, he decided to present Mrs. Hayes with a Siamese kitten, the very first to be sent to the United States. In a letter to the First Lady he wrote:

Dear Madam:

Having observed a few months ago in an American newspaper a statement that you were fond of cats, I have taken the liberty of forwarding to you one of the finest

The morally austere Rutherford Hayes and his wife Lucy pose with their dog and a friend.

specimens of Siamese cats that I have been able to procure in this country. Miss Pussy goes to Hong Kong whence she will be transhipped by the Occidental & Oriental line, in charge of the Purser, to San Francisco and then sent by express to Washington. I am informed that this is the first attempt ever made to send a Siamese cat to America.

I am

> *Very Respectfully*
> *David B. Sickels*

Miss Pussy survived the arduous journey and arrived safely in the White House. The puritanical Hayeses must have found her name too racy, however, for they changed it to Siam. This exotic feline endeared herself to the entire Hayes family and Lucy recorded in her diary: "The Siam cat gaining ground daily in our affections." But Siam's life in the White House was to be a short one. Within a year she was stricken with a serious illness, and on October 1, 1879, Siam passed on to her eternal rest.

The Hayeses were also given a particularly handsome greyhound whose days were numbered. "Yesterday we received by express a beautiful brindle, mouse colored greyhound called Grim," President Hayes noted in his diary. "He is said to be two years old. He is good-natured and neat in his habits." Hayes went on to note that the new arrival had put the other dogs' noses out of joint but that Grim's "social qualities and talents quickly established good relations with them." Unfortunately Grim overestimated his importance and positioned himself in the tracks of an oncoming train. "The death of Grim has made us all mourn," wrote a saddened President Hayes. "He was a great ornament to our house. . . . The whole country knew him, and respected him."

Lemonade Lucy, so nicknamed because of her refusal to serve alcohol at the White House, here feeding pigeons in the snow.

JAMES GARFIELD
MORE BARK THAN BITE, 1881

James Garfield was president for a brief nine months before he was assassinated, and therefore managed to achieve very few of his political goals. However we can get a rough idea of his plans from the name he bestowed on his dog, Veto. Garfield also appears to have had a particularly silly sense of humor when it came to animals. While president he attended a reading given by Charles Dickens. When Dickens recited the words, "Bless his heart: it's Fezziwig again!" from *A Christmas Carol,* a dog in the building responded with a grand series of barks, bringing the house down and amusing Dickens so much he had difficulty continuing. The moment passed quickly enough, but Garfield never seemed to tire of it. For months afterwards, whenever he met anyone who had attended the Dickens lecture, the president of the United States greeted them loudly, howling, "Bow! Wow! Wow!"

The Garfields relaxing with their fish. During his very brief term—he was assassinated after only nine months in office—Garfield kept few animals in the White House.

When he became president after Garfield's assassination, **CHESTER ALAN ARTHUR** (1881-85) was viewed by many as a mysterious figure. To solidify this reputation, his papers disappeared after his death, so no trace of any of his pets—and little of his politics—survives.

The staid Grover Cleveland surprised the country when he married his lively ward Frances, almost thirty years his junior and a great lover of animals. Cleveland poses here with their son Richard and a handsome family dog.

GROVER CLEVELAND
TO MOVE A MOCKINGBIRD, 1885–89, 1893–97

Although Grover Cleveland was a popular and hardworking president, he managed to lose his bid for a re-election in 1888 when the Electoral College over-rode the popular vote. But in 1892, after missing a term, he was elected again to become the only president to serve two non-consecutive terms.

As hard as Cleveland toiled, he also had an eye for beauty, as the country discovered when he married his ward, Frances Folsom, who was almost thirty years his junior. The lively Frances was a great lover of animals and owned a Japanese poodle, several canaries, and a mockingbird. Once when the conscientious president was laboring late into the night, his work was disturbed by the singing of Frances's mockingbird. The president summoned an aide, Thomas Pendel, and asked him to remove the bird. When complete silence followed, Cleveland began to worry that the mockingbird might be sitting in a draft and in danger of catching a cold, so he summoned Pendel again and had him move the bird to a different location. But again the president worried, and again the bird was moved—and again and again. In the end Pendel spent most of the night transferring the mockingbird from one location to another, attempting to soothe the only-too-conscientious Cleveland.

BENJAMIN HARRISON
GETTING HIS GOAT, 1889–93

With his pointed beard and inscrutable eyes, Benjamin Harrison looked remarkably like a goat. And although an austere character, Harrison gave his grandchildren as many pets as they wanted, including a real goat named Old Whiskers. The children created a home for him in the stables, but on his first meeting with Willis, the coachman, the goat charged and cornered him on top of a fence. When he was finally rescued, Willis issued an ultimatum—either the goat went or he did. The diplomatic president worked out a compromise whereby Old Whiskers stayed, but in a new home other than Willis's stables.

Harrison probably should have listened to his coachman. One day while the president was waiting for his carriage on the North Portico, Old Whiskers decided to seek greener pastures and, with the three grandchildren in the cart, took off through the White House gates. Harrison set off in pursuit holding on to his top hat and waving his cane, but the goat happily flouted presidential authority and continued on its way, only halting after Washington residents had seen the chief executive panting and howling after a runaway goat cart.

Harrison's generosity toward his grandchildren extended beyond the gift of Old Whiskers to include a dog named Dash and two opossums named Mr. Reciprocity and Mr. Protection, the latter two of which were later donated to the zoo. The family's

In addition to drawing up elaborate plans that would have quadrupled the size of the White House, First Lady Caroline Harrison made this drawing of her grandchild Baby McKee lounging with a family dog and a cage of birds.

menagerie was completed with four Kentucky thoroughbreds: Abdullah, Billy, Lexington, and John. Harrison himself, however, seems to have had some trouble distinguishing one animal from another. While on a hunting expedition in Maryland, he shot a pig because he thought it was a racoon.

Several members of Benjamin Harrison's family lived in the White House with him, including his daughter Mary McKee and their rambunctious dog Dash.

William McKinley's foreign policy relied heavily on gunboats as he led the country into the Spanish-American War. However his parrot charmed people with old-fashioned diplomacy. Given to the president by a friend, the bird, Washington Post, was described by a newspaper as "a Mexican, double-yellow-headed parrot" (probably not meaning two-headed), and was reported to be worth several thousand dollars. Washington Post's cage was prominently placed in the White House and he chattered to everyone who came by. Whenever a group of women walked past, no matter what their age, the wily old bird would cock its head to one side and cry, "Oh, look at all the pretty girls." The feathered diplomat also managed to charm the president. McKinley claimed Washington Post was the most intelligent bird he had ever met. "That parrot could complete almost any ordinary song I'd hum, sing or whistle," he claimed. "If I began a few bars of 'Yankee Doodle' or 'America,' and then stopped, the parrot would finish the song."

While the president carried on with the affairs of state, his sickly wife, Ida, stayed upstairs in her room crocheting slippers, although she still managed to exercise power in her own fashion. When her Angora cat gave birth to four kittens, Ida named them after prominent figures of the day, including the two weaklings of the litter whom she named Valeriano Weyler, after the governor of Cuba, and Enrique DeLome, after the Spanish ambassador in Washington. According to newspapers: "The President has done

considerable smiling over the matter, and his usual grave demeanor at the Cabinet meeting frequently has given place from time to time to an amused chuckle." But when events in the war with Spain took another downward turn, the kittens were the first casualties. Ida handed Weyler and DeLome to her maid, with strict orders that they be drowned immediately.

Shortly before he was assassinated in Buffalo in 1901, William McKinley, second from right, gazes over Niagara Falls, an anonymous black dog haunting his steps.

The Roosevelts in their summer whites pose with a bright-eyed and noble dog.

Theodore, Jr., with the family's blue macaw, Eli Yale. Eli's favorite food was coffee grounds.

THEODORE ROOSEVELT
THE ROUGH RIDER, 1901–9

After William McKinley's sober administration, Theodore Roosevelt and his clan hit the White House like a cyclone. As the youngest president ever to assume office, Roosevelt had six children and more animals than the White House had ever seen. Among their pets were a small bear named Jonathan Edwards, a lizard named Bill, guinea pigs named Admiral Dewey, Dr. Johnson, Bishop Doane, Fighting Bob Evans, and Father O'Grady, Maude the pig, Josiah the badger, Eli Yale the blue macaw, Baron Spreckle the hen, a one-legged rooster, a hyena, a barn owl, and Peter the rabbit.

The president enjoyed the pets as much as the children. "Jonathan, the piebald rat, of most friendly and affectionate nature, crawls all over everybody," he wrote in a letter, "and the flying squirrel, and two kangaroo rats; not to speak of Archie's pony, Algonquin, who is the most absolute pet of them all." Algonquin was so beloved and so spoiled that once, when the president's son Archie was sick in bed, his brothers Kermit and Quentin brought the pony up to his room in the elevator. But Algonquin was so captivated by his own reflection in the elevator mirror that it was hard to get him out.

The Roosevelt dogs were just as varied, among them Sailor Boy the Chesapeake retriever, Jack the terrier, Skip the mongrel, and Pete, a bull terrier who sank his teeth into so many legs that he had to be exiled to the Roosevelt home in Long Island. Teddy's daughter Alice also owned a small black Pekingese named

Archie Roosevelt and his beloved pony Algonquin on the White House grounds. Once when Archie was ill his brothers brought the pony up to his room in the elevator.

Teddy among the haystacks with two of the Roosevelt dogs.

The rustic Teddy relaxing in rags with a happy lap dog for company.

Manchu, whom she received on a trip to the Far East from the last empress of China. Manchu lived with Alice for several years and she once claimed to have seen it dancing on its hind legs in the moonlight on the White House lawn.

And then there were the snakes. Once when returning from vacation, Quentin stopped at a pet store and bought four snakes. At the White House he found his father in the West Oval Office holding an important meeting. Senators and party officials smiled tolerantly when the boy barged in and hugged his father, but when Quentin dropped his new pets on the table, all hell broke loose. While the officials scrambled for safety, the snakes started to fight with each other. Eventually the president and his son captured them and sent them back to the pet shop.

Alice had a bit more luck with her snakes, at one point owning a green garter snake that she named Emily Spinach ("because it was green as Spinach and as thin as my Aunt Emily"). But stories multiplied about Emily until the word out was that Alice was keeping a giant boa constrictor in the White House. Friends refused to let her visit, until eventually Alice found Emily Spinach dead in its box lying in a highly unsnakelike position—the victim, she was convinced, of a snake assassination.

The Roosevelts' felines were also a force to be reckoned with, particularly a cat named Tom Quartz who terrorized Jack the terrier as well as many human visitors. One evening Joseph G. Cannon, speaker of the House, was leaving the White House after a meeting with the president. Roosevelt escorted him to the head of the stairs and wished him good night. "He had gone about halfway down when Tom Quartz strolled by, his tail erect, and

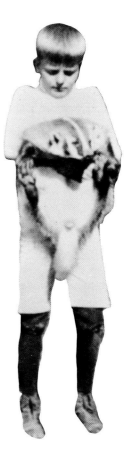

Archie Roosevelt holding Josiah the badger, just one of the family's many exotic pets.

Although the children made a crutch for the Roosevelts' one legged chicken, it seemed to prefer hopping about on its one leg.

very fluffy," President Roosevelt later described the event. "He spied Mr. Cannon going down the stairs, jumped to the conclusion that he was a playmate escaping, and raced after him, suddenly grasping him by the leg the way he does Archie and Quentin when they play hide and seek with him; then loosening his hold he tore downstairs ahead of Mr. Cannon, who eyed him with iron calm and not one particle of surprise."

The Roosevelts also owned a six-toed cat called Slippers, an independent beast who came and went as he pleased but always managed to be back in time for a big party. One evening after an important dinner, the president, with the wife of an important ambassador on his arm, led his guests from the State Dining Room to the East Room. Suddenly the procession of distinguished ambassadors and ministers halted. There on the carpet, right in the path of the president and guests, lay Slippers, luxuriously stretched out full length. Roosevelt's first inclination was to move the cat, but he realized that this would hold up the line and cause a disconcerting pause. So he simply bowed to the lady on his arm and escorted her around Slippers. All the others followed as the whole diplomatic corps gave way to feline comfort.

WILLIAM HOWARD TAFT
THE LAST COW IN THE WHITE HOUSE, 1909–13

The heaviest man to hold the office of president, William Howard Taft was a lover of fine food and fresh milk, and when he came to the White House he brought along his own cow. Mooly Wooly became the first cow in the executive mansion since Andrew Johnson's many years before, but her milk proved unsatisfactory and she was soon replaced by Pauline Wayne, a handsome Holstein who became the last cow in the White House. So devoted was Taft to Pauline and her offerings that a man was hired exclusively to look after the cow and every day he brought her milk to the White House kitchen. When Taft had the old stables torn down, Pauline Wayne was moved along with the elegant presidential cars to a new building at 19th and B streets. But she continued to return to the White House to graze on the grassy slopes behind the War and Navy Building; "She is led there in a dewy morning," reported the *Evening Star*, "and taken away in the twilight."

The biggest appetite ever to be elected president, portly William Howard Taft poses here with his wife, daughter, and their two dogs.

Though many would disagree, Pauline Wayne was the last cow in the White House. The personal milk source of William Howard Taft, she grazed peacefully on the White House grounds, here in front of the Old Executive Office Building.

WOODROW WILSON
MAKING THE WORLD SAFE FOR MAN AND BEAST, 1913–21

Few presidents were as removed from the world of farms and animals as the bookish, intellectual Woodrow Wilson. Nevertheless the bespectacled professor brought a ram called Old Ike to the White House during World War I. As part of the war effort, Ike and his herd kept the lawns cropped while the gardeners went off to make the world safe for democracy. Although Wilson never established a strong relationship with Old Ike, he did occasionally wander through the herd, patting a head here, a back there. And Ike soon became a popular figure, mainly because of his habit of chewing tobacco. Rarely was he seen without a wad clenched firmly between his teeth, the juices running down his chin. But he was neat—unlike others who shared his habit, Ike simply swallowed the wad when he had extracted all the nicotine.

By 1920 the war was over and efforts like having sheep mow the lawns were no longer necessary, so Wilson gave the herd to a Mr. Probert from the Associated Press. Probert sent them to his farm in Maryland where Old Ike's nicotine habit grew worse. He constantly begged for tobacco and picked up the stubs of Probert's cigars. Ike lived on the farm for many years and a bit of him later returned to the White House in the form of a blanket Probert had made from Ike's wool. By 1927, however, Old Ike had grown too old to rise from the ground and had to be put to sleep. Probert gave him one last wad of tobacco and then dispatched him, Old Ike the nicotine addict dying as he had lived.

During World War I Woodrow Wilson brought a flock of sheep to the White House to trim the lawns while the soldiers went off to war. Most prominent among the flock was Old Ike, a ram addicted to tobacco.

The president who made the world safe for democracy judging an international array of roosters at the White House.

Shortly before moving to the White House the Wilsons had lived in a house with a garden filled with songbirds. Although they delighted the family, the birds thrilled their white cat Puffins even more, and every day the lawn was littered with fresh feathers and bones. The Wilsons debated the problem and realized that they would have to choose between the birds or Puffins. But while they agonized, the birds took on the situation themselves. Hearing a loud racket in the garden one morning, the Wilsons rushed outside and found that hundreds of birds had formed delegations in separate trees, flitting back and forth as if in consultation while Puffins crouched in the center of the lawn, ears back, yellow eyes ablaze. Suddenly, as if by Hitchcockian direction, the various groups of hitherto peace-loving songbirds gathered into one huge flock and dove straight for their tormentor. Puffins dashed for shelter under the steps where she stayed for two days, and is said never to have killed a bird again.

WARREN HARDING
THE BEST OF THE WORST, 1921–23

Although Warren Harding is generally regarded as the worst president ever, the reputation of his Airedale, Laddie Boy, is without blemish. Laddie Boy's inauspicious arrival at the White House gave no indication of the important role he was to play in American politics, but before long he was sitting in on cabinet meetings in his very own chair, receiving numerous invitations to important functions, and—quite possibly his finest hour—leading the Humane Society's "Be Kind to Animals" parade through Washington. Laddie Boy was interviewed by the *Washington Star*, the paper reporting his opinions on everything from politics to working hours for guard dogs. The Hardings even arranged a birthday party for him and invited all the neighborhood dogs to celebrate with a cake consisting of layered dog biscuits topped with icing.

But even Laddie Boy was unable to hold the Harding administration together. Troubles such as the Teapot Dome scandal were piling up when Harding died under mysterious circumstances in San Francisco. Rumors circulated about the cause of his death, and when Mrs. Harding refused to allow an autopsy, suspicion ran rampant. Only Laddie Boy remained above reproach. According to Associated Press reports: "There was one member of the White House household today who couldn't quite comprehend the air of sadness which overhung the executive mansion. It was Laddie Boy, President Harding's Airedale friend and companion.

On July 17, 1921, the Washington Star printed a mock interview with Laddie Boy that ran for an entire page and featured two cartoons (including this one). Laddie gave his opinions on everything —Woodrow Wilson's sheep, Prohibition, and the Harding cabinet, and he advocated an eight hour working day for guard dogs.

Overleaf, Laddie Boy was by far the most famous of Warren Harding's pets, a charming Airedale who did much—but not enough—to distract the public from the blossoming Teapot Dome scandal.

Coming to the White House a rawboned, callow pup, Laddie Boy has, in two years, grown to the estate of dignity and wholesome respect for his official surroundings."

After Harding's death, Louis Newman of the Newsboys' Association began a movement to have a statue made of the celebrated Laddie Boy and asked every newsboy in the country to donate one penny to the fund. After Laddie nobly endured fifteen sittings, the 19,134 donated pennies were melted down and molded into a statue by a sculptor named Bashka Paeff. Unfortunately, before the statue could be presented to Mrs. Harding, the former First Lady died, so it went instead to the Smithsonian, where it still stands.

Below left, Warren Harding stoops to pat a pug of remarkably similar appearance. Though a terrible president Harding was a great fan of dogs, and as a newspaperman he sometimes devoted editorials to animal welfare issues.

Below right, a White House policeman makes a wary gesture at one of the Harding turkeys.

CALVIN COOLIDGE
THE COOLIDGE COLLECTION, 1923–29

Calvin Coolidge was so tight-lipped that he earned the nickname "Silent Cal," although he seems to have had no trouble communicating with animals. It's almost impossible to list the creatures that he and his wife, Grace, kept at the White House—indeed their love of animals became so well known that some people shipped their unwanted pets to the president. Between state gifts, presents from friends, and donations from the general populace, the Coolidges received cats, dogs, birds, a raccoon, a baby bear, a wallaby, a pair of lion cubs, an antelope, a large white goose (Enoch), a donkey (Ebenezer), a pigmy hippo, and, from one of the most staunchly Republican counties in America, a snarling bobcat. Most of the wilder gifts were sent directly to the zoo.

Coolidge grew to love Rebecca the raccoon in particular. He had a special house built for her, visited her every day, and even walked her around the White House on a leash. When the White House was being repaired, the First Family moved to temporary quarters near Dupont Circle, but Coolidge worried that Rebecca might be lonely and sent a limousine to bring her from the White House. The president spent several hours playing with the raccoon and then boarded her temporarily at the zoo until they could all move back home together. Later he began to worry that Rebecca might be missing the companionship of the other raccoons, so he found her a mate named Horace. But Horace hated the presidential digs and escaped as soon as he could.

Silent Cal Coolidge stands proudly in front of the White House with Andrew Mellon, his wife Grace, and their elegantly dressed dog Prudence Prim, 1926.

For her part, Grace loved birds and kept a flock of them, including two warbling Harz Mountain canaries named Nip and Tuck, Snowflake the white canary, Old Bill the thrush, a parrot, and a mockingbird. She hated to see birds caged and always set them free in the White House, although her mynah bird's penchant for perching on one of the maid's heads while she did the housework proved to be a problem. The parrot caused trouble in more verbal ways. When the zoo needed money, the White House staff decided to use the parrot to play a trick on the president, and so as Coolidge was preparing for a meeting with the zoo's budget director, a maid prodded the parrot, which screamed on cue, "What about the appropriation!?"

In the realm of more traditional pets, the Coolidges also had three cats—Blackie, Tiger, and Bounder. Blackie dearly loved to ride in the White House elevator, and, after waiting patiently by the door until someone opened it, reclined on the padded seat for hours. Blackie's princely status was readily acknowledged by the president, who treated him with due respect. At one of his breakfasts for politicians Coolidge carefully poured his coffee and cream into a saucer and a few of his guests politely did the same, waiting for the president to take the first sip. But Coolidge smiled, leaned over, and put the saucer on the floor for Blackie.

Tiger, Blackie's companion, didn't take to Washington life so easily, however, and after a while he ran away. Turning to the new medium of radio, Coolidge broadcast a description of the missing cat over the air waves, and he was located and returned. But Tiger knew his own mind, and when he left again not even radio could bring him back. Though he must have sometimes

First Lady Grace Coolidge cuddles Rebecca the raccoon. President Coolidge adored Rebecca and walked her around the White House on a leash.

regretted it Bounder stayed closer to home, where President Coolidge revealed a playful side of his nature by hiding poor Bounder in out-of-the-way places. Alerted by the cat's muffled cries, Grace would rescue him—from bureau drawers, cupboards, and once from a grandfather clock.

While the Coolidge cat population was relatively restrained, the family's dogs seemed to increase without number. Keeping track of them is especially difficult because Grace frequently changed their names. Laddie Boy's half brother, Laddie Buck, lived with the Coolidges, although Grace changed his name to Paul Pry because she said he had his nose in everyone's business. The dog population also included Tiny Tim, who grew up to become Terrible Tim, Blackberry and Ruby Rough the chows, a brown collie named Boston Beans, Peter Pan the terrier, King Kole the bulldog, Bessie the yellow collie, and Palo Alto, a bird dog.

Rob Roy, a white collie originally called Oshkosh, became Cal's favorite dog. Once during a news conference the collie began to whine loudly, and Coolidge snapped at the reporters, "Will you newspapermen kindly keep your big feet off my dog's toes?" Another white collie named Prudence Prim was Grace's favorite. She made large floppy hats trimmed with ribbons for her, which Prudence wore to garden parties. But in the summer of 1926, while accompanying Grace on a trip to the Black Hills of South Dakota, Prudence fell ill and died. Two years later the president's beloved Rob Roy also died.

To help the Coolidges forget their loss, two children sent them a Shetland sheepdog named Diana of Wildwood. She came by plane, in those days not the cleanest way to travel. The first

Grace Coolidge stoops to adjust the hat she made for her elegant white collie Prudence Prim.

Cal communing with a cow.

newspaper reports described her as a black-and-white spotted dog; however when Grace washed Diana she found a white dog under the grime and renamed her Calamity Jane.

At every meal when the president yelled, "Supper," Calamity Jane and all the White House dogs would dash to the elevator and follow him to the dining room where they lounged about during the meal. One guest was not impressed. Describing his dinner with the Coolidges, Will Rogers wrote: "Well, they was feeding the dogs so much that at one time it looked to me like the dogs was getting more than I was. The Butler was so slow in bringing one course that I come pretty near getting down on my all fours and barking to see if business wouldn't pick up with me."

HERBERT HOOVER
PLAYING POSSUM, 1929–33

When Herbert Hoover was running for president, his advisors worried that he was too cold to win public support. And so thousands of copies of this friendly shot of Hoover with his dog King Tut were distributed in a successful attempt to woo the electorate.

Herbert Hoover was a politician with little natural warmth, and as he began his presidential campaign in 1928 his advisors began to fear that he would appear unelectably stiff and cold. Indeed if it hadn't been for his dog King Tut, Hoover might never have become president. Seizing on a photo of a temporarily warm and friendly Hoover with his handsome dog, his campaign staff circulated the image to newspapers as evidence of the candidate's human appeal and sent thousands of autographed copies to voters. The trick worked, Hoover was elected, and he and King Tut moved into 1600 Pennsylvania Avenue.

Although the rest of the Hoover menagerie rarely made the news, it was certainly substantial on the canine front, including Big Ben and Sonnie the fox terriers, Glen the Scotch collie, Yukon the Eskimo dog, Patrick the Irish wolfhound, Eaglehurst Gilette the setter, Pat the police dog, and Weejie the elkhound, who was often mistaken for a pony by people peering through the White House fence. King Tut, however, remained in the public eye. Once in the White House, Tut unfortunately took his guard-dog duties too seriously, driving himself to distraction and eventually becoming known as "the dog that worried himself to death." Every night he patrolled the fences, stopping at each gate and checkpoint. It soon became obvious that the strain was too much for him. Tut became morose, sulked, and lost weight, until finally Hoover sent him back to his house on S Street. There poor puzzled Tut pined away and soon died.

Hoover's affection for his dogs was sincere, but he also seems to have cared for other, stranger animals. At one point he found an opossum on the White House grounds and grew quite attached to it. Meanwhile, in Hyattsville, Maryland, an opossum team mascot named Billy was discovered to be missing. Despite the fact that the Hyattsville-to-D.C. trek would have been daunting for a little opossum, when the boys saw a picture of Hoover and his pet in the newspapers they decided it must be theirs. A delegation went to the White House to identify the animal, but it refused to present itself for inspection and stayed hidden in the kennels. So the boys left a note for President Hoover asking him for the opossum to protect their team from any bad luck that might befall them without their mascot. The president obliged and that year the school's baseball team reached the state championships.

President Hoover, his wife Lou, and King Tut in a relaxed moment at Camp David.

When this opossum wandered onto the White House grounds, President Hoover adopted and even grew quite fond of it.

FRANKLIN DELANO ROOSEVELT
IN DEFENSE OF FALA, 1933–45

The arrival of Franklin Delano Roosevelt transformed political life in Washington, and the pets the Roosevelt family brought with them did likewise. Elliot Roosevelt's dog Blaze hit the headlines when he bumped a homeward-bound soldier off a plane. Meg bit newspaperwoman Bess Furman on the nose. Wink satisfied a profound passion for bacon by stealing it from every available breakfast tray. Dutchess refused to be housebroken and fondly fouled one particular White House rug over and over. And Major, unable to forget his training as a police dog, clamped his jaws onto the arm of every guest. The excessively protective Major overstepped his bounds by taking a bite out of Senator Hattie Caraway's leg, and finally when he ripped the trousers off of British prime minister Ramsay MacDonald he was sent into exile at the Roosevelt home in Hyde Park.

But the Roosevelt dog who achieved the most elevated place of all was Fala. Born on April 7, 1940, and first named Big Boy, Fala was given to FDR by his cousin Margaret Stuckley and his name was changed to Murray of Fala Hill after a famous Roosevelt ancestor. So beloved was the president's Scottie that Roosevelt rarely went anywhere without him. When Winston Churchill and FDR signed the Atlantic Charter in 1941 on the U.S.S. Augusta in the mid-Atlantic, Fala was there at the feet of the two world leaders.

The American public admired Fala, too. In the summer of 1944, the dog and his presidential master went to Hawaii on board the cruiser Baltimore, but during the journey Roosevelt noticed

Above, the very young FDR and his dog in a strange two-seated wicker saddle. Roosevelt's love of animals appears to have been congenital— his mother Sara sent postcards to her dogs when she was away from home.

Left, Fala, the best loved and most famous of all First Pets, with his devoted presidential master. Roosevelt took the little Scottie everywhere, which sometimes resulted in controversy.

that Fala was missing. When he finally located him he was shocked to find that Fala had lost much of his hair, the result, he discovered, of Fala having been enticed below by the sailors, who had plucked tufts of his hair to send to their family and friends.

Fala made headlines in a big way during the 1944 reelection campaign. A rumor was circulated that when Fala had been left behind on the Aleutian Islands, a destroyer had been sent specially to fetch him. FDR's opponents pounced on the story, claiming that Fala had cost the taxpayers thousands of dollars, but with typical aplomb Roosevelt turned the rumor to his advantage. "These Republican leaders have not been content with attacks on me, my wife, or on my sons," he intoned in one of his famous fireside speeches. "No, not content with that, they now include my little dog, Fala. Well of course I don't resent such attacks, and my family doesn't resent attacks, but Fala does. You know Fala is Scotch and being a Scottie, as soon as he learned that the Republican fiction writers in Congress and out had concocted a story that I had left him behind on the Aleutian Islands and had sent a destroyer back to find him at a cost to the taxpayers of two or three, or eight or twenty million dollars—his Scotch soul was furious. He has not been the same dog since."

When Roosevelt died in Georgia a few months after his fourth inauguration, Fala seems to have sensed it back at the White House. On the day of the death, the dog had been dozing in a corner of the room when suddenly he hopped up, ran to the door, and bashed his head against the screen. The screen broke and Fala, crawling through, ran snapping and barking onto a hill where he reportedly sat for hours all alone.

Fala at the feet of the mighty. When the Atlantic Charter was signed on board the Augusta, Fala was there with Winston Churchill and President Roosevelt.

HARRY TRUMAN
TREATING THEM LIKE ANIMALS, 1945–53

Harry Truman earned his nickname "Give 'em Hell Harry" because of the way he treated his opponents, and he seems to have regarded most animals with a similar disdain. During his stay in the White House several animals tried to break into the tight Truman family circle, but in the end they all failed. Early in his term a woman from Missouri sent the president a cocker spaniel puppy named Feller, but Truman gave the pup to the White House physician, Brigadier General Wallace Graham. This snub angered dog lovers throughout the country and Feller's fate became the big news item of the day.

While campaigning in 1948, supporters gave Truman a goat, which they christened Dewey's Goat after Truman's opponent.

Though no cat lover, Truman offers cake to two mystified kittens.

Margaret Truman strolling in front of the White House with one of the family's temporary pets, this one an Irish setter named Mike.

A large cat known as Mike the Magicat also tried and failed. When he first wandered into the White House uninvited, the staff fed and pampered him, afterward sending him home in a chauffeur-driven limousine to the address on his collar. Of course Mike returned, and again he was sent back by limousine. But when a newspaper reporter got hold of the story it was discovered that the cat belonged to the famous seer Jeane Dixon. Thereafter whenever Mike visited the White House, the limousine was foregone and the staff simply called Dixon to come get her cat.

Another Mike was more successful, at least for a little while. A gift from Postmaster General Bob Hannigan to Margaret Truman, Mike the Irish setter seems to have had problems outgrowing his puppyhood and his friskishness soon became too much for the Trumans. Because the police fed him candy he also developed rickets, and with that final straw the Trumans gave him to a farmer in Virginia.

Well known for his stubborn nature,
Harry Truman liked the company of
like-minded animals.

DWIGHT DAVID EISENHOWER
AT WAR WITH IKE, 1953–61

Opposite, the pig Ike received from Elden Holsapple of Indiana never moved into the White House, preferring to stay down at the Eisenhowers' Gettysburg farm.

The Eisenhower era was one of peace and prosperity, but inside the gates of the White House the truce did not always prevail. When the Eisenhowers first moved to the White House they came with two dogs, a Wiemaraner named Heidi and a Scottie called Spunky. Heidi was a rather temperamental animal who didn't care to see Mamie being photographed and would jump up on the First Lady when anyone pointed a camera at her. She was also clearly not cut out for indoor life. One Sunday morning Chief White House Usher J. B. West received a frantic call from Mrs. Eisenhower saying, "Mr. West can you come down right away, we have a terrible problem in the Diplomatic Room." West rushed to the White House and found Mamie wringing her hands. "Heidi," she explained, pointing to two housemen on their knees scrubbing a big yellow spot in the brand-new carpet. All the men in the White House were summoned, and though they moved the furniture and the carpet several times they were unable to hide the stain. The very next day the rug was sent out to be dyed and Heidi was sent to the Eisenhower farm in Gettysburg.

If the interior of the White House suffered from the habits of animals, the grounds took a beating too. President Eisenhower had a putting green in which he took great pride, and every morning he had the gardeners flick the dew off the grass with fishing poles. The squirrels loved it too, digging holes and raising little mounds to hide their nuts. "The next time you see one of those squirrels on

Above, while in North Africa during World War II as Supreme Commander of the Allied Forces, Eisenhower had two Scotties, Telek, a gift from Kay Summersby, and Caacie.

Eisenhower and his Wiemaraner, Heidi, were often on opposite sides of the fence, especially after Heidi misbehaved and had to be banished to Pennsylvania.

my putting green, take a gun and shoot it," Eisenhower thundered at his valet. But the Secret Service stepped in and insisted that shooting on the White House grounds would cause a scandal in the newspapers. Instead they came up with a better solution known as Operation Squirrel Seduction, which involved setting aside a small plot for the squirrels next to the putting green and covering it with peanuts and other delectibles. The squirrels loved their new patch of ground, but they continued to dig up Ike's putting green, so the Secret Service went back to the drawing board and came up with Operation Exodus. This time all the squirrels around the White House were captured and transported to the vicinity of the Lincoln Memorial, but most of them found their way back to the White House. Finally, in the ultimate test of Secret Service wiles, the squirrels were retrapped and taken to Rock Creek Park near Silver Spring. They never came home again.

JOHN FITZGERALD KENNEDY
THE LOT IN CAMELOT, 1961–63

As the second youngest president ever elected, John Fitzgerald Kennedy brought along his children and as many animals as the White House could hold when he moved into the executive mansion. Soon after arriving, First Lady Jacqueline designed a play-yard beneath the trees near the president's West Wing office, with living spaces for the family's rabbits, lambs, ponies, and guinea pigs, and there the president would often escape from the pressing cares of state.

Not content with their original menagerie, once in the White House the Kennedys began to expand on the collection. After a showing of Walt Disney's *Bambi* for Caroline and her friends, Jacqueline asked Chief Usher J. B. West if he could get a deer for the White House Lawn. But before West had a chance to go on a deer hunt, Caroline received two of the animals from Eamonn deValera, the president of Ireland. When West called the National Zoo to inquire about the care of deer, however, he was informed that they could be temperamental and dangerous, so the Irish deer were sent to the zoo.

Kennedy greeting a deer.

Several other Kennedy animals also departed the White House, one way or another. Caroline's cat Tom Kitten preferred the company of the president, which caused problems for Kennedy's allergies. So Tom Kitten was sent to live with the first lady's secretary, Mary Gallagher, and grew up to be Tom Terrific. A pair of hamsters named Billy and Debbie were even more difficult. When Debbie gave birth to six little hamsters, Billy ate them up.

Then Debbie attacked Billy and ate him, and shortly afterwards she sickened and died. The family's birds were slightly less of a problem, the parakeets Bluebelle and Maybelle living happily in their cages, although the canary Robin died and was buried with great pomp on the South Lawn.

But it was the dogs who claimed the most attention. When the Kennedys arrived they brought along Charlie, a Welsh terrier who was nephew of the dog that played Asta in *The Thin Man.* Charlie was soon joined by Pushinka, a gift to Caroline from Nikita Khrushchev and the daughter of Strelka, one of the first dogs in space. Soon after she arrived, Pushinka was taken to Walter Reed Hospital and subjected to a battery of tests carried out behind closed doors by the Army. Both the Army and the White House hotly denied that Pushinka was being checked out for hidden microphones, germs, or a bomb, but Cold War suspicions remained.

Dogs continued to appear, including a German shepherd named Clipper that Jacqueline received from her father-in-law, Joseph Kennedy. Not long after Clipper's arrival, new city dog licenses were issued. Charlie, of course, held onto the #1 tag, but when Pushinka and Clipper were given the #2 and #3 slots, relegating Vice President Lyndon Johnson's dog to #4, a ripple ran through status-conscious Washington. Much more ominously, the two dogs of FBI Director J. Edgar Hoover were demoted to the #5 and #6 slots.

Having failed with the deer, Ireland's Eamonn deValera tried again in the dog vein, this time presenting the Kennedys with an Irish spaniel named Shannon. Another Irish dog also arrived on the scene, this one an Irish wolfhound who was predictably named Wolf. And to top off the canine collection, Charlie and Pushinka

The Kennedys and six of their dogs relaxing during a summer vacation in Cape Cod; dogs, clockwise from upper right, Clipper the German shepherd, Charlie the Welsh terrier, Wolf the Irish wolfhound, Shannon the Irish spaniel, and Pushinka's puppies.

Opposite, Macaroni the pony roamed freely around the White House grounds and received thousands of letters from an adoring public.

Above, Pushinka was the most famous of all the Kennedy dogs. Daughter of Strelka, the first dog in space, she was given to Caroline by Nikita Khrushchev—but only after being thoroughly checked by the Army, which vigorously denied that it was searching for bugs.

had an affair that produced four handsome puppies—Butterfly, White Tips, Blackie, and Streaker. To find homes for them the White House ran a letter-writing contest, with the pups going to the child who best described how he or she would look after them. Had one writer remembered to include his address, his letter might have had a better chance of winning. "I will raise the dog to be a Democrat," he wrote, "and bite all Republicans."

When it came to horses, the Kennedys did themselves proud. Jacqueline and the children loved to ride—the First Lady on a bay gelding called Sardar, given to her by President Auyb Khan of Pakistan, Caroline on her pony Macaroni, a present from Lyndon Johnson, and John, Jr., on his shaggy-maned Conemara pony Leprechaun, yet another offering from the fawning Eamonn DeValera. Although LBJ also gave Caroline another pony, this one appropriately named Tex, it was Macaroni who became something of a national hero, receiving thousands of letters from his young fans. The pony created such a lovely sight as he pulled the children in a sleigh around the White House that a photo of them was used on a family Christmas card. Although the ponies usually stayed at the Kennedy's estate in Virginia, often they were brought to the White House where they freely roamed the South Lawn. One day, at work in his office, Kennedy looked up and saw Macaroni peering at him through the window. After staring at each other thoughtfully for a few minutes, the president opened the window and invited the pony inside. But Macaroni simply turned and ambled away.

LYNDON BAINES JOHNSON

LIVING WITH HIM AND HER, 1963–69

Opposite, when LBJ picked up his beagles by the ears, dog-lovers were enraged.

After the shock and grief of Kennedy's assassination, Lyndon Baines Johnson brought a touch of wry humor to the national stage. Before becoming president, the outspoken Texan had owned a dog he called Little Beagle Johnson—"It's cheaper if we all have the same monogram," he explained. Little Beagle grew up to become Old Beagle, and when he died Johnson had him cremated. For a while the dog's ashes were stored on top of the refrigerator until finally Johnson gave in to his cook's objections and sent the remains to be buried at his Texas ranch.

When LBJ moved into the White House he brought along two new beagles known as Him and Her. In a typically Texan move, the new President took one look at the White House doghouse and immediately ordered that a bigger one be built. Every time Johnson showed the design to a friend, however, the doghouse grew more ambitious and elaborate until finally something of a dog palace was built suitable for a true Texan dog.

During his first few months as president, Johnson scored highly in the popularity polls, but in April 1964 an incident involving Him and Her sent his ratings plummeting. At a meeting with bankers Johnson casually picked up both beagles by the ears while cameras clicked away, and the next day the photos were splashed across the front pages of almost every newspaper in the country. Dog lovers were up in arms and demanded an explanation. But Johnson's answer was typically curt: "To make

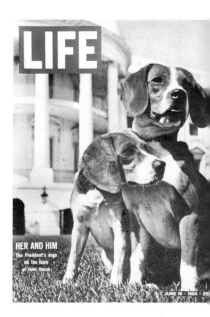

LIFE

HER AND HIM
The President's dogs on the lawn of their house

JUNE 19 · 1964 · 25

Above, the Johnson beagles Him and Her were often in the news, even making it onto the cover of Life.

them bark," he snapped, "it's good for them." No dog lover himself, ex-president Harry Truman came to Johnson's defense. "What the hell are the critics hollering about?" he shrugged. "That's the way to handle hounds."

Him won lasting fame by being the first First Dog to attend his master's inaugural parade, and in other regards as well Him seems to have been favored by LBJ. Women objected when he was assigned D.C. dog license tag #1 and Her received #2, a situation that hardly improved when the licensing department explained that Him was male and therefore the boss. But the beagles' years in the White House were short-lived. Her died on the operating table in November 1964 while vets were trying to remove a rock she had swallowed, and two years later Him was killed by a car while chasing squirrels on the White House grounds.

LBJ in a contemplative mood with Him the beagle and Blanco the neurotic collie.

Him and Her were not the dog-crazy Johnsons' only pets, of course. For several years the family owned a pure white collie they named Blanco, one of a handful of pure white collies in the country and one who fortunately did not suffer from the deafness common to most of her breed. She was, however, highly neurotic, and extremely jealous of any attention the president lavished on Him. To show her displeasure, Blanco once peed on a sculpture by Alexander Calder on loan to the White House from the Museum of Modern Art. Blanco also didn't care very much for another Johnson dog named Edgar, a gift from J. Edgar Hoover, and bit Edgar's nose so badly that he needed stitches.

Despite the presence of so many pure-blooded dogs in the Johnson White House, one of the president's favorite animals was a mongrel called Yuki who had been found by his daughter Luci at a gas station in Texas. Johnson claimed that Yuki spoke with a Texas accent and perhaps for that reason he allowed the little white dog to sit in on cabinet meetings. Once Yuki showed up in the East Room for the signing of a piece of legislation called the Wholesome Meat Act. He wandered around the room and examined everyone present, paying particular attention to a special guest, author Upton Sinclair. On another occasion Yuki showed up at a meeting for top military brass, which the president began by gravely shaking Yuki's paw before he proceeded around the room to shake the hands of the officers.

Yuki listens in while LBJ holds a meeting in the background.

More than any other Johnson dog, Yuki became part of the family—at least in the president's eyes. On the morning of Luci's wedding, as bride, groom, and relatives lined up for a photograph, Yuki wandered in dressed in his best sweater. "We've got to get

Opposite, President Johnson takes a dip with Yuki and grandchild Patrick Lyndon Nugent.

Yuki, a mongrel found in a Texas gas station, was one of President Johnson's favorite dogs.

Yuki in the picture," President Johnson insisted, reaching for the dog. "We can't have a family portrait without him." But Lady Bird didn't agree. Drawing herself up to her full height and looking Johnson straight in the eye, she declared, "That dog is not going in the wedding picture." When the president started to argue, the First Lady commanded the dog keeper, "Mr. Bryant, get the dog out of here right now. He will not be photographed," and Yuki was finally removed. Later while waiting for her husband to finish his tour of duty in Viet Nam, Luci wrote Yuki's biography. "I don't know when it will get published," she admitted, "but I just had to write it. The story of Yuki is part of history."

As the war in Viet Nam played havoc with President Johnson's popularity, he took solace in his standing among his canine supporters. To be on the safe side, however, he kept a box of candy-coated vitamin pills in his desk drawer and doled them out to the eager hounds. Whenever he returned by helicopter to the White House, Johnson also liked to have the unquestioningly supportive dogs on hand to greet him, and as he prepared to land he would eagerly peer out the window to see if the family canines were at the landing pad.

RICHARD NIXON
A CHECKERED PAST, 1969–74

One of the most calculating politicians of the modern era, Richard Nixon recognized early in his career how easily the appeal of animals could be exploited. It was 1952, and things seemed to be going fine with the Eisenhower-Nixon ticket until the papers got hold of a story that Nixon had a secret slush fund of contributions from rich supporters. Years later after he was elected president, Nixon reminisced: "I remembered that Roosevelt had come under attack in 1944 supposedly for sending a destroyer to pick up his dog Fala when it was left behind in the Aleutian Islands. Roosevelt had destroyed his critics by saying, 'I don't resent attacks on my family or on me, but Fala does resent them.'" In his own speech, Nixon also pulled on the heartstrings of animal-loving Americans. While he claimed to have received no major gifts, he did admit that "Someone in Texas had sent us a little black-and-white cocker spaniel puppy. My daughter had named it Checkers. . . . and I said that regardless of what anyone said about it, I was going to keep it." Milking Checkers for a maximum of sentimental appeal, Richard Nixon scuttled the brewing scandal and went on to become vice president.

When Nixon finally moved into the White House as president in 1969, he brought along his two daughters' dogs, Julie's French poodle Vicky and Tricia's Yorkshire terrier Pasha. Shortly after the president's arrival his new staff gave him his own dog, an Irish setter puppy that Nixon named King Timahoe—Timahoe after "the little village in Ireland where my mother's Quaker ancestors came from"

Opposite, if dogs could talk, Vicky Nixon would have much to tell. Here she eavesdrops on a Nixon Kissinger meeting.

Above, without Checkers, Nixon might have been dropped from the vice presidential ticket in 1952.

and King because even for his dogs Nixon seems to have harbored royal ambitions. "If he's the presidential dog he will be treated like a king won't he?" Nixon demanded. "Even a president's dog gets royal treatment." But the American people didn't much care for the King part, and simply called the setter Timahoe.

Timahoe's handshaking became a White House ritual, and he was photographed greeting virtually every dignitary who visited. During one particular photo session, however, Timahoe proved uncooperative and refused to strike a good pose. Nixon's valet, Manolo Sanchez, finally grabbed the dog by the nose and pushed his hindquarters to the ground, the cameras capturing every move. Afterwards the ever-paranoid president panicked, fearing that the photos would show Tim being abused. So after fretting all night, Nixon had his official photographer track down all the photos to see that none were incriminating.

Not exactly a natural around pets, Nixon would sometimes get flustered trying to walk Timahoe. "He would get Timahoe's leash all wadded up in his hands and I would stand there wanting to help him out but not wanting to draw attention to it," remembers Chief White House Dog Keeper Traphes Bryant. "And sometimes in his nervousness, he would just chuck the wadded-up mess to me." Timahoe himself was a model of decorum and so were the other dogs—with the exception of Vicky the poodle's unfortunate habit of chasing the goldfish in the fish pond. But Timahoe, Vicky, and Pasha were to follow their master into exile after Nixon's resignation, the only dogs in history to be hounded from the White House because of their master's misdeeds.

According to the Audubon Society, in 1969, at the beginning of

Though models of decorum themselves, the Nixon dogs were hounded out of the White House because of their master's pranks.

Nixon's first term, the White House grounds were home to three cardinals, six mockingbirds, a woodpecker, a blue jay, a crow, a robin, 69 house sparrows, 85 starlings, and one pigeon. Although Nixon did not have a close relationship with any of them, at least he let them alone. Before his 1972 inauguration parade, on the other hand, on the new president's orders, Pennsylvania Avenue was sprayed with chemicals to keep the pigeons away.

A rare moment of relaxation:
Richard Nixon with poodle Vicky.

Ford's gregarious golden retriever Liberty was always on hand in the Oval Office should the president need canine advice.

G ERALD F ORD
GIVE HIM LIBERTY, 1974–77

After the sordid mess of Watergate, Gerald Ford did all he could to restore the reputation of the presidency. When the Fords first moved to the White House they brought along their Siamese cat Chan, and to enhance their clean mid-western image they soon added a dog to the family circle. A gift from official White House photographer David Kennerly, the golden retriever puppy Liberty became close friends with the president, and together they provided the press with countless photo opportunities—swimming, playing, or relaxing. Soon Liberty's photographs were so much in demand that a special rubber stamp of her paw print was made, which Susan Ford herself imprinted onto the shots before sending them out. Liberty even helped Ford with his political business. When visitors lingered too long in the Oval Office, the president signaled the dog, who would rush in and provide a diversion that would allow the president to bring the conference to a close.

When Liberty was about to have pups she was moved from her usual kennel to a room on the third floor where she could be near her trainer. One evening the trainer had to go out, so the job of walking Liberty fell to the President. Awakened by a wet kiss at about 3 A.M., Ford put on slippers and robe and went downstairs with Liberty. When she had finished her business they returned to the house. But when Ford pressed the button for the elevator nothing happened. The president climbed the stairs to the second floor, but to his dismay he found the door to the family quarters

Susan Ford and her Siamese cat Chan.

Betty Ford and Liberty check out the retriever's pups. One of them, Jerry, went on to become a guide dog for the blind.

was also locked, and so was the door on the third floor. After walking up and down the stairs several times the irate Ford started pounding on the walls. The White House sprang alive, lights came on everywhere, and the Secret Service rushed to the scene to let the president back into his own house.

*Gerald Ford and family feed a deer
named Flag at Camp David.*

JIMMY CARTER
TRUE GRITS, 1977–81

As a boy growing up on his family's peanut farm in Plains, Georgia, Jimmy Carter had owned a dog named Bozo and a horse called Lady Lee. But in 1977 when it was time to move to the White House, the family menagerie consisted solely of a Siamese cat called Misty Malarky Ying Yang. Not long after, however, Amy Carter's public school teacher gave her a puppy, and that puppy became the mortal enemy of the cat.

In true Southern fashion, Amy named her dog Grits. But Grits had difficulty adapting to life with the Carters and Misty Malarky Ying Yang. He *did* allow his medical exam to be photographed in front of the White House to promote Heartworm Awareness Week. But when a vet placed a muzzle on him before drawing blood, Grits decided his civic-mindness had gone far enough and he tore off the muzzle with his paws, forcing the vet to pretend to draw blood for the cameras. Unwilling to bend to the protocols of White House pet behavior and unable to stop chasing Misty Malarky Ying Yang, Grits was soon returned to his original owner.

Carter's animal connections were not limited to the domestic variety, however—indeed one of the most memorable moments of his entire presidency involved a wild rabbit. During the spring of 1979 while fishing from a boat in a pond near Plains, President Carter spied what he described as "a fairly robust-looking rabbit" swimming towards his boat. The strange aquatic rabbit seemed intent on joining the president in the boat, but Carter shooed it

Amy Carter and her Siamese cat Misty Malarky Ying Yang. During most of the Carter term this cat reigned supreme as the one-and-only First Pet.

Amy Carter and Grits strike a
pensive pose. Their friendship was
short lived, doomed by Grits's
friskiness and his adversarial
relationship with Misty Malarky
Ying Yang.

away with his oar. Before long the story hit the headlines.
PRESIDENT ATTACKED BY RABBIT ran on the front page of the
Washington Post, and for weeks afterwards the story was covered
by every paper and network. Some journalists criticized the
president for being too timid and merely shooing the animal away
while others thought he was too brutal. And others still raised the
burning question—what was a rabbit doing in a pond, and why
was it so aggressively pursuing the president? For weeks the
country debated the rabbit issue, but nobody seemed to think that
perhaps this was simply an animal striving to become a First Pet.

RONALD REAGAN

DESIGNER DOGS, 1981–89

Washington went Hollywood when Ronald Reagan was elected president, and glitz became the order of the day in every aspect of life. Although for the first years the Reagans were dogless, finally in 1985 they acquired a canine with a suitable image and pedigree—a tiny nine-week-old sheepdog named Lucky. The cuddly pup grew and grew until within a few months she stood more than two feet tall and weighed almost eighty pounds. When the First Lady walked her, a White House staff member commented, "At times it looks like Mrs. Reagan is water skiing or skateboarding behind the dog. There is a real fear she's going to fall down." But Nancy Reagan was not going to risk falling and breaking her hair, so she sent Lucky for five weeks of obedience training. When this didn't help, Lucky was sent to live at the Reagan's Santa Barbara ranch, joining a long and honorable line of dogs exiled from the White House.

Ever attuned to the power of media and not one to miss the great photo opportunities afforded by a dog, Reagan then replaced Lucky with Rex, a one-year-old King Charles spaniel. Although a little easier to handle, Rex too pulled on his leash, often dragging the Reagans away from reporters and photographers before anyone had a chance to ask the president questions about how he was running the country.

To ensure that Rex lived in surroundings no less lavish than his presidential owners, the Washington Children's Museum commissioned a doghouse for him. For this important job they

*Above, although Reagan usually
prepared his best face for
photographers, Rex was caught a
little off guard here.*

chose Theo Hayes, an interior designer married to a descendent of nineteenth-century president Rutherford B. Hayes. "It's very colonial," Hayes said of her doghouse design. "White clapboard with a cedar shingle roof. I didn't do it feminine or prissy. It's not as if I was doing it for a French poodle or a chihuahua. There are draperies of red fabric . . . and on the wall are pictures of Ron and Nancy in acrylic frames."

Rex's life as First Dog had a true Hollywood ending, for as Reagan rode into the sunset at the end of his term, Rex followed faithfully along to frolic poolside in Bel Air.

Ronald Reagan motivating his horse with a carrot-like incentive.

G EORGE B USH
THE MEDIA HOUNDS, 1989-NOW

After eight dutiful years as vice president under Reagan, George Bush finally took over the top job in 1989 and moved into the White House. By then his dogs Mildred Kerr and C. Fred Bush had become old Washington hands, well able to manipulate the media. Both Millie and Fred grabbed the limelight for themselves by writing autobiographies, and *Millie's Book* became one of the bestsellers of 1990. When Millie had puppies she appeared on the cover of *Life,* but celebrity did not lead her to neglect her maternal duties—she found good homes for her pups, especially Ranger, who now lives with Bush granddaughter Marshall and is a regular visitor at the White House.

But not all the media attention has been favorable. Even before *Millie's Book* came out, *Washingtonian* magazine had voted Millie "Ugliest Dog" and put her picture on their cover. Later the magazine apologized and sent dog biscuits as a peace offering, which President Bush accepted on Millie's behalf in a letter to editor Jack Limpert. "Dear Jack," he wrote. "Not to worry! Millie, you see, likes publicity. She is hoping to parlay it into a Lassie-like Hollywood career. Seriously, no hurt feelings: but you are sure nice to write. Arf, arf, for the dog biscuits. Sincerely, G.B."

Following the runaway success of her autobiography, Millie's health problems then grabbed headlines. At first it was thought that she was suffering from lead poisoning, but later vets decided that she had Lupus—an extremely rare disease in a dog, and rarer still considering that Millie, the president, and Barbara Bush were all

Goerge Bush prancing with Ranger, one of Millie's puppies.

Opposite, George and Ranger gazing out to sea from the Maine coast.

suffering from the same ailment. All three were duly hospitalized, treated, and released, but the deepest national sigh of relief came when Press Secretary Marlin Fitzwater grandly announced, "Millie's in good shape and back performing her functions as First Dog." Those functions—from providing unquestioned support to enhancing the presidential image—have changed little during the two hundred years that the White House has played host to a host of presidential pets. And as the latest in a long line of White House wildlife, Millie has been mindful of the importance of her role. Frolicking with the ghosts of countless presidential cats and dogs, birds and snakes, cows and horses, not to mention alligators, tigers, opposums, wildcats, turkeys, badgers, raccoons, and pigs, Millie has proudly taken her place among the distinguished ranks of First Pets.

Millie and Ranger patiently waiting for the president to knock off for the day.

ALLIGATOR
John Quincy Adams

ANTELOPE
Calvin Coolidge

BADGER
Theodore Roosevelt

BEAR
Thomas Jefferson
Theodore Roosevelt
Calvin Coolidge

BIRD
Canary
Rutherford B. Hayes
Grover Cleveland
Calvin Coolidge
John F. Kennedy
Chicken
Theodore Roosevelt
Woodrow Wilson
Eagle
James Buchanan
Gamecock
Andrew Jackson
Ulysses S. Grant
Goose
Calvin Coolidge
Mockingbird
Thomas Jefferson
Rutherford B. Hayes
Grover Cleveland
Calvin Coolidge
Mynah bird
Calvin Coolidge

Owl
Theodore Roosevelt
Parakeet
John F. Kennedy
Parrot
George Washington
James Madison
Andrew Jackson
Ulysses S. Grant
William McKinley
Theodore Roosevelt
Calvin Coolidge
Partridge
Thomas Jefferson
Peacock
Thomas Jefferson
Pheasant
Thomas Jefferson
Pigeon
Rutherford B. Hayes
Thrush
Calvin Coolidge
Turkey
Abraham Lincoln
Warren Harding
Unknown species
Benjamin Harrison
Woodrow Wilson

BOBCAT
Calvin Coolidge

CAT
Angora
William McKinley

Siamese
Rutherford B. Hayes
Gerald Ford
Jimmy Carter
Unknown species
Theodore Roosevelt
Woodrow Wilson
Calvin Coolidge
Harry Truman
John F. Kennedy

COW
William Henry
Harrison
Andrew Johnson
William Howard Taft
Calvin Coolidge

DEER
Thomas Jefferson
John F. Kennedy
Gerald Ford

DOG
Airedale
Warren Harding
Beagle
Lyndon B. Johnson
Bird Dog
Calvin Coolidge
Bulldog
Calvin Coolidge
Bull Terrier
Theodore Roosevelt
Chesapeake Retriever
Theodore Roosevelt

Chow
Calvin Coolidge
Cocker Spaniel
Harry Truman
Richard Nixon
Collie
Calvin Coolidge
Lyndon B. Johnson
Elkhound
Herbert Hoover
English Mastiff
Rutherford B. Hayes
Eskimo Dog
Herbert Hoover
Fox Terrier
Herbert Hoover
French Hound
George Washington
German Shepherd
John F. Kennedy
Golden Retriever
Gerald Ford
Greyhound
Rutherford B. Hayes
Irish Setter
Harry Truman
Richard Nixon
Irish Spaniel
John F. Kennedy
Irish Wolfhound
Herbert Hoover
John F. Kennedy

Italian Wolfhound
John Tyler
King Charles Spaniel
Ronald Reagan
Newfoundland
James Buchanan
Ulysses S. Grant
Pekingese
Theodore Roosevelt
Police Dog
Herbert Hoover
Poodle
Grover Cleveland
Richard Nixon
Scotch Collie
Herbert Hoover
Scottie
Franklin D. Roosevelt
Setter
Herbert Hoover
Sheepdog
James Monroe
Calvin Coolidge
Ronald Reagan
Spaniel
James Monroe
Terrier
Theodore Roosevelt
Calvin Coolidge
Welsh Terrier
John F. Kennedy
Wiemaraner
Dwight D. Eisenhower

Yorkshire Terrier
Richard Nixon
Unknown Species
George Washington
James Garfield
Benjamin Harrison
Theodore Roosevelt
Franklin D.Roosevelt
Lyndon B. Johnson
Jimmy Carter
George Bush
DONKEY
Calvin Coolidge
ELEPHANT
James Buchanan
FISH
James Garfield
Richard Nixon
GOAT
Abraham Lincoln
Rutherford B. Hayes
Benjamin Harrison
Harry Truman
GUINEA PIG
Theodore Roosevelt
John F. Kennedy
HAMSTER
John F. Kennedy
HIPPO
Calvin Coolidge
HORSE
George Washington
John Adams

Andrew Jackson
John Tyler
James Polk
Zachary Taylor
Ulysses S. Grant
Benjamin Harrison
Franklin D. Roosevelt
John F. Kennedy
Ronald Reagan
HYENA
Theodore Roosevelt
JACKASS
George Washington
LAMB
John F. Kennedy
LION
Calvin Coolidge
LIZARD
Theodore Roosevelt
MOUSE
Andrew Johnson
MULE
George Washington
Franklin D. Roosevelt
OPPOSUM
Benjamin Harrison
Herbert Hoover
PIG
Abraham Lincoln
Theodore Roosevelt
Dwight D. Eisenhower
PONY
Abraham Lincoln

Ulysses S. Grant
Theodore Roosevelt
John F. Kennedy
RABBIT
Abraham Lincoln
Theodore Roosevelt
John F. Kennedy
Jimmy Carter
RACCOON
Calvin Coolidge
RAT
Piebald
Theodore Roosevelt
Kangaroo
Theodore Roosevelt
SHEEP
James Madison
Woodrow Wilson
SILKWORM
John Quincy Adams
SNAKE
Theodore Roosevelt
SQUIRREL
Theodore Roosevelt
Dwight D. Eisenhower
TIGER
Martin Van Buren
WALLABY
Calvin Coolidge

INDEX

Adams, John, 14
Adams, John Q., 17, *17*
Algonquin (T. Roosevelt's pony), 49, *49*
Arthur, Chester Alan, 41

Blackie (Coolidge's cat), 62
Blanco (L. Johnson's dog), 84, 85
Blaze (F. Roosevelt's dog), 69
Bounder (Coolidge's cat), 63
Buchanan, James, 27
Bush, George, 101–2, *103*
Butcher Boy (Grant's horse), 33

Carter, Jimmy, 96–97
Chan (Ford's cat), 93, *93*
Charlie (Kennedy's dog), 78, *79*
Checkers (Nixon's dog), 89, *89*
Cincinnatus (Grant's horse), 33, *34*
Cleopatra (John Adams's horse), 14
Cleveland, Grover, 42, *42*

Clipper (Kennedy's dog), 78, *79*
Coolidge, Calvin, *60*, 61–64, *64*

Dash (B. Harrison's dog), 43, 44
Diana of Wildwood (Calamity Jane) (Coolidge's dog), 63–64
Dick (Jefferson's mockingbird), 15
Dutchess (F. Roosevelt's dog), 69

Edgar (L. Johnson's dog), 85
Eisenhower, Dwight, *74*, 75–76, *76*
Eli Yale (T. Roosevelt's bird), *48*, 49
Emily Spinach (T. Roosevelt's snake), 51

Faithful (Grant's dog), 33–34
Fala (F. Roosevelt's dog), *68*, 69–70, *70*
Feller (Truman's dog), 71

Fillmore, Millard, 26, *26*
Ford, Gerald, *92*, 93–94
Fred (Bush's dog), 101

Garfield, James, *40*, 41
General (Tyler's horse), 23
Grant, Ulysses S., *32*, 33–35, *34*, *35*
Grim (Hayes's dog), 38–39, *38*
Grits (Carter's dog), 96, *97*

Harding, Warren, 57–59
Harrison, Benjamin, 43–44
Harrison, William Henry, 20, 21
Hayes, Lemonade Lucy, *36*, 37, *39*
Hayes, Rutherford B., *36*, 37–39
Heidi (Eisenhower's dog), 75
Him and Her (L. Johnson's dogs), *82*, 83–84, *83*, *84*
Hoover, Herbert, 65–67, *65*, *66*
Hoover, J. Edgar, 78, 85
Jack (Lincoln's turkey), 30

Jackson, Andrew, 18–19, *18*
Jeff Davis (Grant's horse), 33
Jefferson, Thomas, 14–15, *14*
Johnny Ty (Tyler's canary), 22–23
Johnson, Andrew, 31, *31*
Johnson, Lyndon, 78, *82*, 83–86, *84*, *85*
Josiah (T. Roosevelt's badger), 49, *51*

Kennedy, John F., 77–80, *77*, *81*
King Tut (Hoover's dog), 65, *65*, *66*

Laddie Boy (Harding's dog), 57–59, *57*, *58*
Laddie Buck (Paul Pry) (Coolidge's dog), 63
Lafayette, Marquis de, 13, 17
Lara (Buchanan's dog), 27
Leprechaun (Kennedy's horse), 80
Liberty (Ford's dog), *92*, 93–94, *94*

Lincoln, Abraham, *28*, 29–30

Little Beagle Johnson (Old Beagle) (L. Johnson's dog), 83

Lucky (Reagan's dog), 98

Macaroni (Kennedy's horse), 80, *81*

McKinley, William, 46–47, *47*

Madame Moose (Washington's dog), 12–13

Madison, James, 16

Major (F. Roosevelt's dog), 69

Manchu (T. Roosevelt's dog), 49–51

Meg (F. Roosevelt's dog), 69

Mike (Truman's dog), 72

Mike the Magicat (Truman's cat), 72, *72*

Millie (Bush's dog), 101–2, *102*

Miss Pussy (Hayes's cat), 38

Misty Malarky Ying Yang (Carter's cat), 96, *96*

Monroe, James, 17

Mooly Wooly (Taft's cow), 53

Nanny and Nanko (Lincoln's goats), 29–30

Nelson (Washington's horse), *12*

Nixon, Richard, *88*, 89–91, *89, 91*

Old Ike (Wilson's ram), 55, *55*

Old Whiskers (B. Harrison's goat), 43, *45*

Old Whitey (Taylor's horse), *24*, 25

Pasha (Nixon's dog), 89, 90

Pauline Wayne (Taft's cow), 53, *53*

Pierce, Franklin, 26, *26*

Polk, James, 23, *23*

Poll (Jackson's parrot), 18–19

Prudence Prim (Coolidge's dog), *60*, 63, *63*

Puffins (Wilson's cat), 56

Pushinka (Kennedy's dog), 78, *80*; puppies, *79*, 80

Ranger (Bush's dog), 101, *101, 102, 103*

Reagan, Ronald, 98–100, *98, 99, 100*

Rebecca (Coolidge's raccoon), 61, *62*

Rex (Reagan's dog), 98–100, *98, 99*

Rob Roy (Coolidge's dog), 63

Roosevelt, Franklin D., *68*, 69–70, *69, 70*

Roosevelt, Theodore, *48*, 49–52

Royal Gift (Washington's mule), 11–12

Sardar (Kennedy's horse), 80

Shannon (Kennedy's dog), 78, *79*

Slippers (T. Roosevelt's cat), 52

Sukey (W. H. Harrison's cow), 21

Taft, William Howard, 53, *53*

Taylor, Zachary, *24*, 25

Tex (Kennedy's horse), 80

Tiger (Coolidge's cat), 62

Timahoe (King) (Nixon's dog), 89–90

Tom Kitten (Tom Terrific) (Kennedy's cat), 77

Tom Quartz (T. Roosevelt's cat), 51–52

Truman, Harry, 71–72, *72, 73*, 84

Tyler, John, 22–23, *22*

Van Buren, Martin, 19

Veto (Garfield's dog), 41

Vicky Nixon (Nixon's dog), *88*, 89, 90, *91*

Washington, George, *10*, 11–13, *13*

Washington Post (McKinley's parrot), 46

Weejie (Hoover's dog), 65

Wilson, Woodrow, 55–56, *56*

Wink (F. Roosevelt's dog), 69

Wolf (Kennedy's dog), 78, *79*

Yuki (L. Johnson's dog), 85–86, *85, 86, 87*

PHOTOGRAPHY CREDITS

Sources of photographic material and photographers are as follows:
Jimmy Carter Presidential Library: pp. 96, 97; Dwight D. Eisenhower Presidential Library: pp. 74, 75, 76; Gerald Ford Presidential Library: pp. 8, 92, 93, 95; Benjamin Harrison Home: pp. 43, 44; Rutherford B. Hayes Presidential Center: pp. 36, 39; Lyndon B. Johnson Presidential Library: pp. 6, 82, 84 (Frank R. Wolfe), 85 (Y. R. Okamoto), 86 (Y. R. Okamoto), 87 (Y. R. Okamoto); John F. Kennedy Library: pp. 2-3, 77, 79, 81; Martin Luther King Branch, Washington, D.C., Public Library: p. 94; Library of Congress: pp. 1, 5, 10, 12, 13, 14, 15, 16, 18, 20, 24, 28, 32, 34, 35, 40, 42, 45, 47, 48 top, 49, 50 top, 52, 53 top and bottom, 54, 56, 58, 59 left and right, 62, 63, 64, 65, 66, 67, 108; *Life* magazine/Francis Miller: p. 83; New York Historical Society: p. 33; New York Public Library: p. 17, 22, 23, 26 left and right, 31; Richard M. Nixon Presidential Library: pp. 81, 88, 89, 90; Ronald Reagan Presidential Library: pp. 98, 99, 100; Franklin D. Roosevelt Presidential Library: pp. 69, 70; Theodore Roosevelt Collection, Harvard College Library: pp. 48 below, 50 below; Harry Truman Presidential Library: pp. 71, 72 top, 73; UPI/Bettmann Archive: pp. 60, 68, 72 below, 80, 89, 101; White House: pp. 102, 103.

ACKNOWLEDGMENTS

I would like to express my most sincere thanks to all those without whom this book would not have been completed: the people at the various presidential homes, libraries, and museums for patiently anwering all my questions; the staff at the Library of Congress; Betzy Iannuzzi and Don Rieck for introducing me to Abbeville Press; Cathy Mahar for her invaluable advice; Celia Fuller for her marvelous design; my editor Constance Herndon for believing in the book and keeping it alive; and of course Joseph Coencas for his support throughout this process.